CHOCTAW

Heather Bruegl

21st Century
Junior Library

Indigenous Peoples
of North America

Published in the United States of America by:

CHERRY LAKE PRESS
2395 South Huron Parkway, Suite 200, Ann Arbor, Michigan 48104
www.cherrylakepress.com

Reading Adviser: Beth Walker Gambro, MS, Ed., Reading Consultant, Yorkville, IL

Photo Credits: © Katie Hadley Photography, cover, title page; © Moab Republic/Shutterstock, 5; © AP Photo/The Oklahoman, Jaconna Aguirre, 6; © AP Photo/Rogelio V. Solis, 9; © wjarek/Shutterstock, 11; NASA image enhanced by BobNoah/ Shutterstock, 13; © TLF Images/Shutterstock, 14; © AP Photo/Alonzo Adams File, 17; US Department of Agriculture via Flickr, 19; © David Creedon/Alamy Stock Photo, 21

Cherry Lake Press is an imprint of Cherry Lake Publishing Group.

Library of Congress Cataloging-in-Publication Data has been filed and is available at catalog.loc.gov.

Cherry Lake Publishing would like to acknowledge the work of the Partnership for 21st Century Learning, a network of Battelle for Kids. Please visit Battelle for Kids online for more information.

Printed in the United States of America

Note from publisher: Websites change regularly, and their future contents are outside of our control. Supervise children when conducting any recommended online searches for extended learning opportunities.

About the Cover: Beckah Boykin of Choctaw Nation served as consultant and model for a feature in *Brides of Oklahoma* (now Wed Society Oklahoma) magazine called "A Vibrant Tradition: A Walk Through the Choctaw Wedding Aesthetic." The feature produced the image shown on the cover as well as others that highlight Choctaw wedding traditions. Boykin works as a model and actress. She is also a Choctaw social dancer, hymn artist, and stickball player.

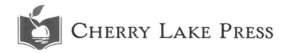
CHERRY LAKE PRESS

CONTENTS

WHO WE ARE

The Choctaw people call themselves *Chahta*. They are an Indigenous group. The land that is now the United States has been their home for thousands of years. The Choctaw people value faith, family, and culture. They recognize a deep connection among all living things. As with many Indigenous groups, Choctaw elders help preserve culture and knowledge. The Choctaw use this knowledge to grow and prosper.

The Choctaw Nation of Oklahoma is the third-largest tribe in the United States.

The Choctaw language is an important part of Choctaw life. It is important to Choctaw identity. The language keeps them connected to their ancestors. It helps them connect with future generations.

The Choctaw language was first written down just a few hundred years ago. It uses a version of the Latin alphabet like English does.

Think!

What does being a good neighbor mean to you? How can you work to be a good neighbor in your life?

Choctaw values also include being a good neighbor. Through fairness and service, the Choctaw believe in strength through togetherness.

Choctaw culture grows and changes. It builds on past traditions. For example, stickball is a popular Choctaw sport. Traditionally, it helped settle arguments between families. Today, the World Series of Stickball is a championship tournament. The sport might even help settle arguments between nations.

Choctaw basket making, pottery, storytelling, art, and dance are all traditions that thrive today. The skills and art forms are passed down from generation to generation. Each artist combines modern ideas with traditional methods. This adds layers to the rich and vibrant Choctaw culture. It is a culture that is very much alive today.

There are three **federally recognized** Choctaw bands. These are the Choctaw Nation of Oklahoma, the Mississippi Band of Choctaw Indians, and the Jena Band of Choctaw Indians in Louisiana. Each band shares a common culture and language, but each has its own history and government.

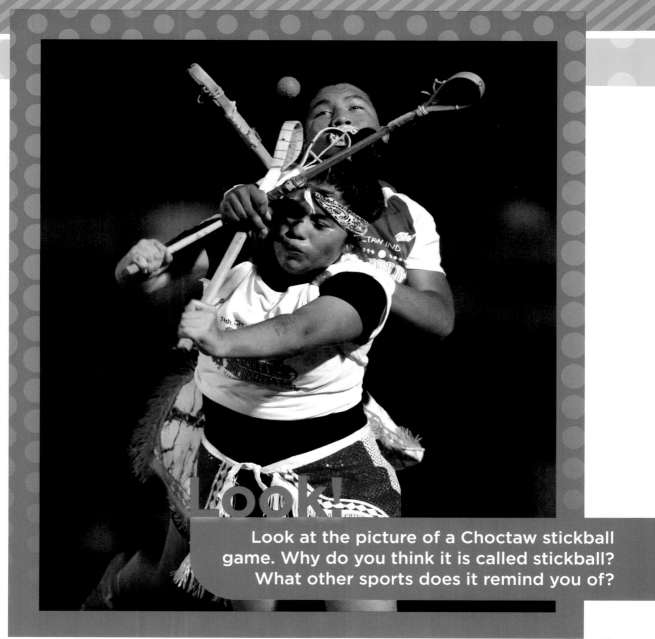

Look!

Look at the picture of a Choctaw stickball game. Why do you think it is called stickball? What other sports does it remind you of?

OUR LIVES TODAY

Today, most Choctaw people live in Oklahoma and Mississippi. Each of the three Choctaw tribal nations has its own reservation. The largest is in southeastern Oklahoma. It is home to the Choctaw Nation of Oklahoma. It is around 11,000 square miles (28,490 square kilometers). Many Choctaw also live on the Mississippi and Louisiana reservations.

Choctaw people are an important part of American life. They contribute to many fields, including the arts and sciences.

Jeffrey Gibson is a Choctaw/Cherokee artist and sculptor. His work, shown here, has been displayed around the world.

In 2023, **heirloom** Choctaw seeds traveled to space! These seeds were saved for generations. They were sewn into clothes. This kept them safe on long journeys. These seeds represent America's oldest crops. Scientists will study how these seeds grow in space.

Choctaw sacred lands in Mississippi are still important. One such place is the Choctaw Mother Mound. It is called *Nanih Waiya* or the "slanted mound." Choctaw tradition says this is where the Choctaw began. This land was lost in a treaty with the United States. But in 2008, this sacred land was returned to the Mississippi Band of Choctaw.

Choctaw seeds on the
International Space Station

Create!

Research ancient mounds in Mississippi and
Alabama. Choose three. Create a travel
brochure with facts and images that guide
visitors along a route to visit all three.

Choctaw communities thrived in these lands for generations, and some still do today.

OUR ANCESTRAL LANDS

The Choctaw people originally called the southeastern United States home. Their lands covered parts of Mississippi, Louisiana, and Alabama. The land was rich and fertile. The Choctaw were expert farmers. They farmed in the Three Sisters method. They planted corn, beans, and squash. They grew other crops such as sunflowers. They also gathered berries and other edible wild plants. They sometimes grew more than they needed. They traded extra crops with neighboring tribes.

The Choctaw took great care of the land. They used controlled burns. This is a type of **forest management**. It helps clear land for new plants. It can also help keep the soil fertile. Along with other Indigenous nations, the Choctaw view the land as a living and breathing being. It is something that must be preserved for future generations.

In 1830, the U.S. Congress passed the **Indian Removal Act**. The Choctaw were forced to leave their homelands. If they didn't, the United States

Make a Guess!

Why do you think the Three Sisters are such important crops? If you said it is because of the complete nutrition they provide, you'd be right!

Gary Batton is the 47th chief of the Choctaw Nation. Choctaw leaders today help defend land and water rights.

threatened to destroy them. The Choctaw signed a removal treaty. This meant they had to rebuild their lives in Indian Territory. That land is part of Oklahoma today. Not all Choctaw left. Some still live on their ancestral lands. Those that did leave faced a hard journey. One-third to one-fourth of Choctaw people died. The Choctaw Trail of Tears was a time of great sorrow.

CARRYING TRADITIONS FORWARD

Choctaw people still remember and honor those lost during removal. Each year, they hold a Trail of Tears Memorial Walk. They remember the journey. They also celebrate how much survivors overcame. Those who survived set up new governments. They built schools. They built farms. The Choctaw Nation became the strongest economy in Indian Territory.

Ask Questions!

What questions do you have about how Choctaw people adapted to change? Find a librarian, teacher, or adult to help you find answers to your questions.

The Choctaw way of life continued. Their spirit of generosity was not defeated. In 1847, the Choctaw learned of the Great Hunger in Ireland. People there were starving. The Choctaw raised what would be $5,000 in today's U.S. dollars. They sent it to the town of Midleton. That is in County Cork, Ireland. The Irish learned the money came from the Choctaw many years later. The Irish people have a history of colonization, too. Their appreciation brought the two peoples together in friendship.

The relationship between the Irish and the Choctaw continues today. It includes scholarships to send Choctaw students to study in Ireland. When the

COVID-19 pandemic started, the Irish organized a fundraising event. They sent the money raised to support not only the Choctaw but also the Diné (Navajo) and Hopi peoples. These peoples were suffering. These donations were in honor of and in thanks for the help the Choctaw gave to the Irish.

This Kindred Spirits monument stands in County Cork, Ireland, in honor of the Choctaw Nation.

GLOSSARY

colonization (kah-luh-nuh-ZAY-shuhn) the act of settling in an area and exercising control over Indigenous peoples

federally recognized (FEH-druh-lee REH-kig-niezd) a status assigned to U.S. tribal nations by the federal government that provides specific rights and benefits

fertile (FUHR-tuhl) full of nutrients and able to support growth

forest management (FOR-uhst MA-nij-muhnt) the act of taking care of forests and wild spaces to encourage growth and health

Great Hunger (GRAYT HUN-guhr) commonly called the Irish Potato Famine; a time in Ireland of great starvation and disease from 1845 to 1852

heirloom (AIR-loom) a plant variety that is unchanged over several generations

Indian Removal Act (IN-dee-uhn rih-MOO-vuhl AKT) a law passed in 1830 that moved tribes living in the southeastern part of the United States to west of the Mississippi

Indian Territory (IN-dee-uhn TAIR-uh-tor-ee) the U.S. area west of the Mississippi River where Indigenous peoples were forced to move; today is the state of Oklahoma

reservation (reh-zuhr-VAY-shuhn) a legally designated plot of land held in trust for Indigenous peoples by the U.S. federal government

Three Sisters (THREE SIH-sterz) a form of planting in Indigenous communities that refers to the planting of corn, beans, and squash

FIND OUT MORE

Books

Bruegl, Heather. *Indian Removal*. Ann Arbor, MI: Cherry Lake Press, 2024.

Sorell, Traci. *We Are Grateful: Otsaliheliga*. Watertown, MA: Charlesbridge, 2021.

Sorell, Traci. *We Are Still Here! Native American Truths Everyone Should Know*. Watertown, MA: Charlesbridge, 2021.

Online

With an adult, explore more online with these suggested searches.

- MBCI World Series Stickball via YouTube

- "School of Language Resources," Choctaw Nation of Oklahoma

Say Hello!

Halito (huh-lee-TOE) is a way to say "hi" in Choctaw.

INDEX

ABOUT THE AUTHOR

Heather Bruegl, a member of the Oneida Nation of Wisconsin/Stockbridge-Munsee, is a Madonna University graduate with a Master of Arts in U.S. History. She is a public historian and decolonial educator, and her Munsee name is Kiishookunkwe, which means "Sunflower in Full Bloom." Heather frequently travels to present on Indigenous history, policy, and activism, bringing her deep knowledge and personal connection to the subject.